Conversations

on

Circling the Sun
By Paula McLain

dailyBooks

FREE Download: Get the Hottest Books!
*Get Your Free Books with **Any Purchase** of Conversation Starters!*

 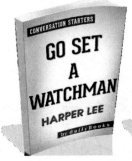 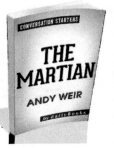

Every purchase comes with a FREE download of the hottest titles!

Add spice to any conversation
Never run out of things to say
Spend time with those you love

Read it for FREE on any smartphone, tablet, Kindle, PC or Mac.
No purchase necessary - licensed for personal enjoyment only.

Get it Now

or Click Here.

Scan Your Phone

Tips for Using dailyBooks Conversation Starters:

EVERY GOOD BOOK CONTAINS A WORLD FAR DEEPER THAN the surface of its pages. The characters and their world come alive through the words on the pages, yet the characters and its world still live on. Questions herein are designed to bring us beneath the surface of the page and invite us into the world that lives on. These questions can be used to:

- Foster a deeper understanding of the book
- Promote an atmosphere of discussion for groups
- Assist in the study of the book, either individually or corporately
- Explore unseen realms of the book as never seen before

About Us:

THROUGH YEARS OF EXPERIENCE AND FIELD EXPERTISE, from newspaper featured book clubs to local library chapters, *dailyBooks* can bring your book discussion to life. Host your book party as we discuss some of today's most widely read books.

Table of Contents

Introducing *Circling the Sun*

CIRCLING THE SUN IS THE FICTIONAL BIOGRAPHY OF BERYL Markham, a woman who pushed the boundaries of society. Markham's life starts in England, but when she was a child, her parents moved to Kenya. Beryl immediately falls in love with the country and the way of life, makes African friends, and adopts African customs. Her mother could not handle the life and returned to England, leaving Beryl with her father. As she grew up, the absence of the restrictive British culture and customs led Beryl to try to push her luck in different ways.

Beryl Markham was one of the first women in Africa to enter the male-dominated industry of horse breeding. As a child, Beryl was very fond of horses and even had one of her own. She quickly learned how to deal with every aspect of horse breeding before she was even an adult. She worked for Lord Delaware in the beginning, but gradually began to be offered different horses to be trained. She achieved triumph in the races, and in spite of the prevalent sexism, she made a name for herself. She became one of the first licensed horse trainers in the continent.

Markham also was one of the first women to complete a solo transatlantic flight. The book shows her journey towards finding a passion for flying, which started by accident, and then developed into a full-fledged passion and career.

Finally, the book also discusses Beryl's marriages, affairs, and sex life in detail, especially her triangle with Denys Finch-Hatton and Karen Blixen. Married off at a young age to a neighbor, she undergoes abuse from him and many other men in her life. Finally, it is when she is alone that she is able to achieve success and fame.

Chafing at the strictures of colonial life in Africa and England, Beryl moves from one milestone to another, exploring places where other women had not even thought to enter. This book takes a look at the troubles women had to face in British East Africa and England in the 1920s and '30s. They had to work twice as hard for only a grudging recognition. Beryl, despite all her troubles and everything stacked against her, overcame it all. The book portrays more of her relationships than her struggles or achievements, but there are hints of the latter as well.

Introducing the Author

PAULA MCLAIN IS AN AMERICAN AUTHOR WHO IS interested in writing about obscure women in history. She picked Hadley Richardson, Earnest Hemingway's first wife, for her first biography and then subsequently wrote about Beryl Markham, a female pioneer of flying, in her next fictional biography. She has also written a memoir about her own experiences growing up in the 60s. She also has two poetry books under her belt. In short, she is a versatile author who has tried her hand at different genres and has received major acclaim for her work.

Born in Fresno, California, in 1965, McLain was abandoned by both her parents. Her mother simply vanished without a word when McLain was four years old, leaving her and her two sisters to fend for themselves. Her father was extremely unreliable as a caretaker and was often in trouble, going in and out of prison during much of her childhood. Though McLain first stayed with family, it didn't work out as a permanent option, and she and her sisters were given over to foster care. Over the next fourteen years, McLain and her sisters were shunted around several foster homes. She has described her ordeals in the book *Like Family: A Memoir*.

When she aged out of the foster system, she began to work odd jobs. Then, she discovered that she could write. She obtained her masters of fine arts in poetry and received several fellowships.

Currently, she lives with her two younger children in Cleveland after having married and divorced twice. Connor, her eldest son, lives in Japan.

Her most popular book to date is *The Paris Wife*, which sold 1.5 million copies. Her works have been translated into more than thirty languages around the world.

Discussion Questions

question 1

A couple of Beryl's friends were into flying at a time when it was a dangerous and expensive sport, meant only for the rash and rich people. In what way would flying have been fascinating to a woman like Beryl in the 1920s?

question 2

Beryl and her friends were all Europeans, and they owned all the
land around. Describe the different ways in which colonialist
attitudes are displayed by Beryl and her friends.

. . . .

question 3

Beryl's mother disliked Africa, whereas her father loved it. Beryl herself couldn't feel at home elsewhere, but her brother was a true Englishman. Why do you think some people are drawn to some places and cultures while others are not?

. . . .

. . . .

question 4

Beryl, on a trip to a family friend's farm, was attacked by a tame lion that the family had raised since he was a cub. After this incident, the lion was caught and locked up. Do you think this was fair? What mistakes did the lion's owners make during this time?

. . . .

question 5

Beryl talks about the tribal chieftain who was sent off to the First
World War to fight a battle in which he or his tribe were never
involved. Why do you think these people went into a battle that
had nothing to do with them?

. . . .

. . . .

question 6

When Beryl's father went bankrupt and had to sell the farm, he practically thrust Beryl into an unwanted marriage with their neighbor, Jock, which quickly went sour. What other options, if any, do you think he had for Beryl's life?

. . . .

. . . .

question 7

Jock liked Beryl when she was riding around the estates, free as a
bird, but the minute they get married, he begins to feel
inadequate and starts acting like a sulky child, especially when it
comes to sex. Why do you think he displayed such a discrepancy
in his attitude?

. . . .

question 8

Beryl's marriage with Jock went sour very quickly. Jock was extremely worried about appearances and wouldn't give Beryl the divorce she wanted. Why do you think Jock thought it worthwhile to hang on to a dead relationship?

. . . .

question 9

Beryl despises her mother for not being able to sleep on damp
sheets or rough it out, unlike her. Is this really a fair thing to
expect of anyone, especially a woman who has no experience of
such things? How do you think this antagonism developed?

. . . .

. . . .

question 10

Denys was a big game hunter who enjoyed hunting the animals in Africa, but when he had to take Vanderbilt and some Americans hunting, he was really annoyed that they killed the animals. Do you think he was being hypocritical or is there something different in the way they hunted? Give reasons for your answer.

. . . .

. . . .

question 11

Jock picked a fight with Lord Delaware at a party, and the brawl
ended with Delaware getting hurt. Beryl got fired even though
she was the one who wanted to bring in the police. Why do you
think people blamed Beryl for an incident in which she wasn't
involved?

. . . .

question 12

Beryl got pregnant and had to have an illegal abortion in England. A friend of her father's paid for it in return for sex. Beryl had to take up the offer, but once they both returned to Africa, Frank induced his friend to rape her, and she only saved herself by locking herself in the bathroom. What legal recourse could Beryl have had during this time and what would her options have been?

· ·

question 13

Beryl and Ruta grew up together even though they were from different worlds. Even as adults, they stuck together, and Ruta always gave Beryl moral support. However, Africans didn't have the same status as the Europeans. Considering this, do you think Beryl and Ruta shared an equal relationship? Give reasons for your reply.

· ·

. . . .

question 14

Berkeley was in love with a Somalian woman, with whom he lived. However, this was kept a secret from the rest of the European society. Why do you think Berkeley felt he had to keep his relationship a secret?

. . . .

· ·

question 15

Mansfield and his mother blamed Beryl's horse riding on her
child being born with problems. Were they justified in doing so?
Give reasons for your answer.

· ·

question 16

Alexandra Fuller wrote a brilliant review of *Circling the Sun* in *The New York Times*, in which she called the book a "bodice ripper." Do you think this is an accurate description of the book? Why or why not?

question 17

The Independent reviewer, Julie McDowall, says that the novel was too ambitious, and the story gathers speed and then lifts off and vanishes. Did you feel the same? Can you point out the shortcomings of the book in this context?

question 18

Jean Zimmerman, in her review in *NPR Books*, says that the author mythologizes crucial incidents in Markham's life. What do you think she means by this? Can you give some examples from the book?

question 19

In her *Daily Express* review, EithneFarry says that *Circling the Sun* is full of dazzling images celebrating the landscape that captured the heart of Beryl Markham. In what way does the book manage to celebrate the landscape of Kenya?

question 20

In her review in *The Dallas Morning News,* Joyce Sáenz Harris claims that the author does not attempt to capture the voice of the more mature Beryl Markham, but depicts the story from the viewpoint of young Beryl. What is your opinion about the voice used in *Circling the Sun*?

FREE Download: Get the Hottest Books!
*Get Your Free Books with **Any Purchase** of Conversation Starters!*

Every purchase comes with a FREE download of the hottest titles!

Add spice to any conversation
Never run out of things to say
Spend time with those you love

Read it for FREE on any smartphone, tablet, Kindle, PC or Mac.
No purchase necessary - licensed for personal enjoyment only.

Get it Now

or Click Here.

Scan Your Phone

. . . .

question 21

In *The Boston Globe*, reviewer MameveMedwed says that *Circling the Sun* is a gift for the hidden adventurer in all of us. To what is she referring, and how does the book bring out the adventurer in the reader?

. . . .

. . . .

question 22

Circling the Sun has often been compared to *Out of Africa*. What
similarities and differences did you see between these two
books?

. . . .

question 23

Laura Albritton claims, in her review for *Miami Herald,* that McLain gives just the right dose of intelligence and self-awareness to her heroine. Do you agree with this? To what extent do you think Beryl made intelligent decisions and was aware of where her decisions were taking her?

question 24

The *Entertainment Weekly* reviewer, Leah Greenblatt, claims Beryl Markham may have married more than once, but she was nobody's wife. What do you think she means by this?

. . . .

question 25

Tom Beer, a reviewer from *Newsday*, says that *Circling the Sun* sidesteps some of the more vexed racial aspects of African colonialism. Do you agree with this statement? Why, or why not?

. . . .

. . . .

question 26

Paula McLain likes writing about historical women. She has
written two books, one about Hadley Richardson, Earnest
Hemingway's first wife, and the other about Beryl Markham. She
also started and abandoned a book about Marie Curie. Why do
you think she is so attracted to these female pioneers?

. . . .

question 27

McLain spent her childhood without any parenting, shunted from one foster home to another. How do you think this affected her life and her writing?

. . . .

question 28

McLain equates her story to a "rags-to-riches" one, saying she spent more than three years doing odd jobs and scraping together money to pay the bills, and then she suddenly had a life of plenty after *The Paris Wife* became a huge success. How do you think this change affected her?

. . . .

. . . .

question 29

McLain received a masters of fine arts in poetry. Do you think
that her education in poetry has contributed anything to the way
she writes her novels?

. . . .

question 30

Paula McLain has written books about different people and on different topics in her writing career. Which one of her books do you think would be best adapted into a movie?

. . . .

question 31

When Beryl's father went bankrupt, he tried to force his daughter to marry the neighbor despite the age difference between them and she was not even slightly interested in him. He didn't tell her that she had about one year to decide and Beryl rushed into a marriage thinking there was no other option. In Beryl's situation, what would you have done?

. . . .

question 32

Beryl's parents moved to Kenya from England as a result of her father's decision. Her mother hated it, and she wanted to return to England, but her father had already invested in the country and loved life there. Beryl's mother finally separated from him and returned to England. If you were in Beryl's mother's position, what would you have done?

. . . .

. . . .

question 33

Beryl got pregnant and had to have an illegal abortion in England. A friend of her father's paid for it in return for sex. The other option was to be a single mother because she was sure that Denys wouldn't be tied down. If you were in that position, what option would you have chosen and why?

. . . .

. . . .

question 34

Mansfield Markham and his mother did their utmost to keep
Beryl away from her son, and because of the laws during those
days, they were able to do so. Beryl had to leave her son behind
when she returned to Africa. What would your choice have been
and why?

. . . .

. . . .

question 35

Beryl was taken to Africa at a young age and considered it home. She became one of the first women to be a licensed pilot and a licensed horse trainer. If Beryl had remained in England, would this have been possible? Give reasons for your answer.

. . . .

. . . .

question 36

Beryl fell in love with Denys even though he was with Karen and was open about not wanting to commit himself to any woman. However, Beryl still wanted to be with him. If you were in Beryl's place, what kind of relationship would you have sought with Denys, if any, and why?

. . . .

. . . .

question 37

Karen had refused to give a divorce to her husband, Blix, for the
sole reason that he wanted to marry another woman and she
would lose her title. She did this despite the fact that she was in a
relationship with Denys that was going nowhere. In Karen's
place, what would you have done?

. . . .

· ·

question 38

Ruta and Beryl had managed to keep their friendship alive despite their different backgrounds merely by accepting the status quo. If you had been in their place, how would you have maintained the friendship and what would your expectations have been from the friendship?

· ·

Quiz Questions

. . . .

question39

True or false: When Beryl moved to Africa as a child, she went to the Colony of Kenya.

. . . .

question40

Karen Blixen wrote a book under the pseudonym of _____.

. . . .

question41

True or false: Beryl had to go to England for an abortion because it was illegal in Kenya.

. . . .

question42

Beryl's best friend was Ruta, a member of the _____ tribe.

question 43

Beryl's biggest triumph on the racecourse was _____.

question 44

True or false: Denys Finch-Hatton taught Beryl to fly a plane.

. . . .

question 45

Beryl's son was named _____.

. . . .

question 46

McLain abandoned a book on _____.

. . . .

question 47

True or false: McLain grew up in foster homes.

. . . .

question 48

McLain's most popular book is _____.

. . . .

question 49

McLain has a masters of fine arts from _____.

. . . .

. . . .

question 50

True or false: McLain has written a memoir about her childhood
lived in foster homes.

. . . .

QuizAnswers

1. False. Beryl moved to the East Africa Protectorate
2. Isak Dinesen
3. False. Abortion was illegal in both Kenya and UK. Beryl didn't know she was pregnant when she went to the UK. Abortion was legalized in the UK only in 1967 and in Kenya in 2010.
4. Kipsigi
5. Wise Child
6. False. Denys never bothered much with Beryl except to quote poetry to her and have sex with her. Tom Campbell Black, another well-known aviator, taught Beryl to fly.
7. Gervaise
8. Marie Curie
9. True
10. The Paris Wife
11. University of Michigan.
12. True

THE END

Want to promote your book group? Register here.

  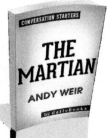

Printed in Great Britain
by Amazon